I0763343

Putrescent Poems

Horror Poetry

Titles Available from Forty-Two Books

Peaks of Madness: A Collection of Utah Horror
Edited by Daniel Cureton and Johnny Worthen

Forthcoming Titles from Forty-Two Books

2019

Strange Stories Vol 1
Edited by Daniel Cureton, Amy Pittman, and Kylie Williamson

Satan Speaks! Contemporary Satanic Voices
Edited by Faustus Blackbook

Monster Brain: Conversations with OCD
by Daniel Cureton

2020

They Walk Among Us: A Collection of Utah Horror by the Utah Horror Writers.

Strange Stories Vol 2

All Titles Available on Amazon.com or from Forty-Two Books

Putrescent Poems

Horror Poetry

Volume 1

October 2019

Edited by Daniel Cureton

and Kylie Williamson

A Forty-Two Books, LLC. original publication,
Salt Lake City, UT, USA
www.fortytwobooks.com
Printed in USA on acid free paper. Upper East Side, AC Mountain, and Times New Roman Fonts.

ISBN-13: 978-1-7340067-2-8
Library of Congress Control
Number: 2019913979

Cover Art by Fernando Cortes—See "Bibliography," page 85.

Editors
Daniel Cureton, MA
www.danielcureton.com
Kylie Williamson

First Edition. First Printing.

LETTER FROM THE EDITORS

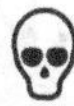

It is with extreme gratitude that we thank all the authors involved in this work. Thank you to all whom took the time to submit to the open call (over 200 submissions!), and worked with us to be accepted up the standard of professional publication. You have our darkest thanks.

In Poetics,
Daniel Cureton,
Kylie Williamson,
October 1, 2019
Salt Lake City, UT, USA

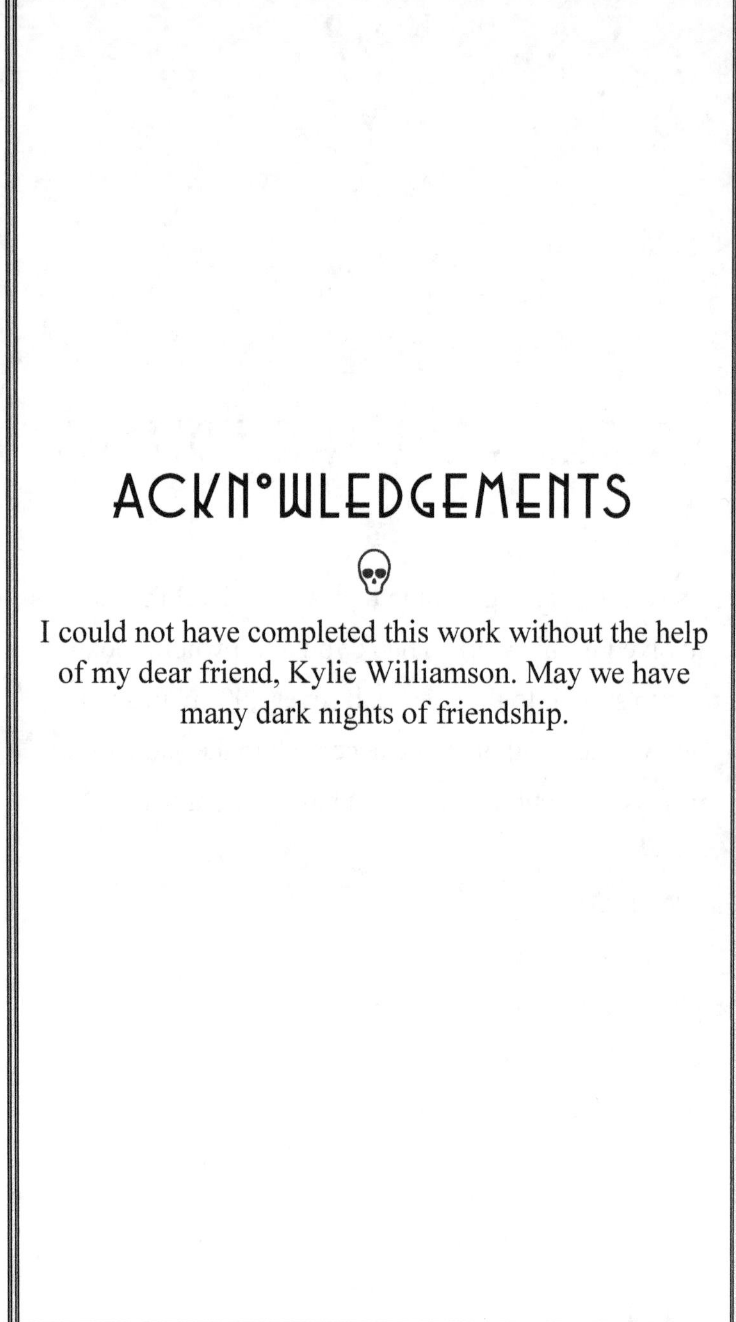

ACKNOWLEDGEMENTS

I could not have completed this work without the help of my dear friend, Kylie Williamson. May we have many dark nights of friendship.

INTRODUCTION FROM THE PUBLISHER

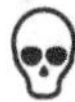

Putrescent Poems was born from my love of writing, literature, and the desire to publish high quality poetry. Horror is often overlooked in many ways as escapist or for the thrill seekers. But horror gives life meaning by placing us against the very things that scare us, challenge us, and force us to consider our place in the universe—so too does poetry. As a fine art, poetry evokes a sense of deep fulfillment in the writing of it and reading of quality craft. Putting horror and poetry together invites the reader to take in deep stimulation, confront boundaries, and to enjoy fresh, unpublished poems from authors from around the world.

I was barely done from publishing *Peaks of Madness: A Collection of Utah Horror* for the Utah Horror Writers when submissions began rolling in. My dear dark friend, Kylie Williamson from graduate school, enthusiastically volunteered to help in the project.

It is the aim of the publisher to present fine, unique, and unpublished poems—regardless of subject matter—which testify to the power of poetry as the art of words. With pleasure I present:

Putrescent Poems

In horror,

Daniel Cureton, MA

Forty-Two Books, LLC.

October 1, 2019

Salt Lake City, UT, USA

REGISTER OF HORRORS

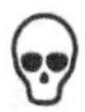

THE HORRORS

AUTHOR BIOGRAPHIES

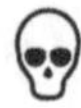

Brian James Lewis is a disabled poet, writer, and book reviewer who feels that writing is as important as breathing. He is a member of the SFPA and has been reviewing dark poetry and speculative fiction since 2016. First published in *Trajectory* in 2014, Brian's work has appeared in *The Toilet Zone* from HellBound Books, *Haunted Are These Houses* from Unnerving, *Bards & Sages Quarterly*, and *Weird Mask Zine*. Find out more at www.damagedskullwriterandreviewer.com

Christina Digan is from Toronto, Ontario and has a background in writing and acting. She loves to travel and run obstacle course races in her spare time. Find out more at www.zenandtheartofswearing.com

Christopher Woods is a writer and photographer who lives in Chappell Hill, Texas. He has published a novel, *The Dream Patch*, a prose collection, *Under a Riverbed Sky*, and a book of stage monologues for actors, *Heart Speak*. His photographs can be seen in his gallery www.christopherwoods.zenfolio.com and his photography prompt book for writers, *From Vision to Text*, is forthcoming from Propertius Press.

David F. Shultz writes speculative fiction and poetry. David is from Toronto, ON, where he is lead editor at tdotSpec, producing anthologies such as *Strange Economics* and *Imps & Minions*. His over fifty published works are featured or are forthcoming through publishers such as Abyss & Apex, Diabolical Plots, and Third Flatiron. Find him online at www.davidfshultz.com

Detroit Kallunki was born in Tuscaloosa, Alabama and raised in Roswell, New Mexico. She is a nineteen year old university student who is being charged far too much money to get take classes on a language that she already knows. She has been writing stories and poems since she could hold a pencil and reading for even longer; literature is definitively her one true love.

Frank Coffman is a retired professor of college English and creative writing. He has published speculative poetry and fiction in a variety of magazines and anthologies. His poetic magnum opus, *The Coven's Hornbook & Other Poems* has been followed by his rendition into English Verse of 327 quatrains of *Khayyám's Rubáiyát*—both from Bold Venture Press and available on Amazon. He selected and edited *Robert E. Howard: Selected Poems*. A member of the Horror Writers Association and the Science Fiction & Fantasy Poetry Association, Frank established and moderates the *Weird Poets Society* Facebook group. See his writer's blog at www.frankcoffman-writer.com

Joanna Koch writes literary horror and surrealist trash.

Author of the novella *The Couvade* and other short fiction, their work has been published in journals and anthologies such as *Synth, Fable, Honey & Sulphur*, and *In Darkness Delight: Masters of Midnight*. Consume their monstrous musings at www.horrorsong.blog.

John Andrews lives in Portsmouth, England and is a lover of music, movies and entertainment all round. Currently finding a voice in story telling, John has several published shorts and a set of kindle poetry books around life with mental health and knowing that world with empathy.

John L. Smith, Jr. is a graduate of Arkansas State University at Beebe. He has written several novels, one textbook, and a translation of an ancient text. His most recent publication is "A World in Stillness Shroud" in *Uncharted*, an online magazine for the campus.

Jordan Paris is a senior high schooler in Connecticut who plans on attending a college in New York City and major in creative writing. He has participated in many writing and journalism opportunities such as writing for Greenwich Free Press and *Affinity Magazine*, as well as creating stories for the *Greenwitch Literary Magazine* school newspaper. He placed top three in the 2015 Virginia Rotary Club Essay Contest. Through his stories, he wants to create a world where awareness is brought to a variety of injustices, bringing the surreal to a world we inhabit.

AUTHOR BIOGRAPHIES

Kurt Newton is the bastard son of three poetic fathers: Dr. Suess, Maurice Sendak, and Edward Gorey. Kurt's verse and lyrical prose have appeared in numerous publications over the past twenty years, including *Weird Tales*, *Space & Time*, *Dreams and Nightmares, Mythic Delirium*, *Polu Texni*, and *Spectral Realms.*

Kylie Williamson is a graduate student in her final year at Weber State University in Ogden, Utah. She has been published in *Enheduanna* and *Utah's Best Emerging Poets,* and presented at the National Undergraduate Literature Conference. She is passionate about writing, teaching, and oxford commas.

Mike Meroney has been writing in one form or another since he was eight years old. His writing education was forged on reading everything he could get his hands on. He loves black coffee and dark beer and is at his happiest when he is creating. Mike has written short stories and poetry for both children and adults and hopes to someday write a novel. He lives in the desert of Arizona with his wife and their dogs.

M. Alan Vreeland is a former English teacher who had an early fascination with the works of Edgar Allen Poe and Agatha Christie. Under an alternate moniker, he is also a singer/songwriter, playwright, and poet. Currently, he lives in upstate New York with his wife and cat. While doing genealogy research, he discovered he is a descendant of a woman who died in jail after being accused of witchcraft during the Salem Witch Trials.

North Adam is 13 different people trying to fit into one permanently baffled brain. She translates for a living and writes to stay sane.

R. K. Wolford writes poetry and tiny stories in the San Francisco Bay area.

Shannon Elizabeth Gardner is a graduate from the University of Wisconsin-Stevens Point with a bachelors in studio art and a minor in art history. Her interest in horror and the macabre came about while exploring nature and the paranormal. She believes life is beautiful when left to fate—leaving art to chance assists the viewer to witness beauty hidden within imperfections. The works included explore the natural and organic process of death, evoking empathy for decay.

Shaun Avery has been published in many magazines and anthologies. He has won competitions with both prose work and comic scripting. A lifelong fan of comics and graphic novels, he is the proud co-creator of a self-published horror comic, found online at Comicsy.co.uk. "Alone in the Land of Robots" is based on his own unfortunate history and general ineptitude around electrical items.

Warren Denbrock Porter found his love of poetry in the butchery of brutal death metal. At 15 he began writing lyrics for bands such as Diminished, Stages Of Decomposition, and Goremonger. The art of writing a small window through which a story can be seen fascinates him. Over the years of living in Michigan and working with bands, he continued to learn about and practice poetry until he found himself overseas studying Creative Writing at Bangor University in North Wales.

THE HORRORS

MASTER OF DECAY

Shannon Elizabeth

Ink on Paper

2018

MASTER °F DECAY

SEDATED PREGNANCY

Warren Denbrock Porter

Oh how long for this moment I have waited,
for when her body lies limp and her heart rate is sedat-
ed.

SEDATED PREGNANCY

Blood is raining from the tip to my shaft,
I relish in the sight of my blasphemous craft.

Orgasms coursing through the blood of my spine,
causing sensations of the utmost divine.

With pale eyes rolling to the back of his head,
soon he will die and no prayers will be said.

The child is hung with the umbilical cord,
without interference from Jesus the Lord.

Gone without a future or dreams,
all that remains are his echoing screams.

From this world his soul has lastly departed,
before his life ever truly got started.

The mother's heart is barely beating,
the soul itself is slowly retreating.

Into the black without a heaven so bright,
your hell for me is a blissful delight.

God is not blessing a second last breath,
he chose for my hands to grace you with death.

I bathe in their silence, for what is dead, is done,
oh my poor lover; oh my poor son.

THE VALDEMAR EFFECT

Frank Coffman

He'd been intrigued by one grim tale by Poe
About a mesmerist and the physical effect—
If one sought the craft of hypnotism to know
And put those skills to use—one could direct
A subject so enthralled to imitate
Symptoms of dread diseases—even Death.
But when he realized it was too late;
The pallor and chill of flesh—yes!
But the breath had ceased now fifteen minutes since,
And ten attempts to end the spell had failed,
He fled that abandoned house and hurried thence,
Back to his flat, dreading what he'd unveiled.

They found him one month later in his bed,
Strangled by hands of flesh fully one month dead!

FIXER-UPPER

M. Alan Vreeland

I took my cue from Frankenstein;
he made his then, now I've made mine.
With offset ears and crooked smile,
mine has a kind of Frankenstyle.

I searched for parts, some hard to get;
I must admit, I've some regret.
One leg so short, from toe to rump;
it's much more like a Frankenstump.

The poor guy's missing his male pair
with not much in his underwear.
In that department, he's a dud,
he'll never be a Frankenstud.

Then there's that whiff of rotting smell,
Gangrenous putrid flesh as well;
with French cologne I spray, then drench,
to cover up that Frankenstench.

FIXER-UPPER

And when he roams the city streets,
he scares the people that he meets;
the strongest men faint when he talks,
so now he hides and Frankenstalks.

I realize now, without a soul
the danger's real, I've lost control!
What have I done? Oh, what a mess!
There's no end to my Frankenstress!

I scream, "I'll lock you in a cage!"
He turns on me with red-eyed rage;
in panicked fright, a knife I grab;
oh yes, I'll do it: Frankenstab.

As he lay dead upon the floor,
I swear I'll create nevermore.
Am I upset? No, not one sniff—
he's as he should be, Frankenstiff.

I hate for flesh go to waste;
I'm curious about the taste.
Well, what else would you have me do,
but have a bowl of Frankenstew.

TELL ME AWFUL THINGS

Kylie Williamson

Tell me awful things

like how your grandpa was butchered
with his own kitchen knife.
A boning knife to be exact.
How he was sitting in his recliner
watching the news with a blanket over
his legs
comforting him.

Tell me how many stabs and slashes
his wrinkled body houses.
Was it 7 or 8? Maybe 10.
Tell me how deep each one is
and which wound was fatal.
Is it the one to his chest?
The sawing of his throat?

Bother me with gruesome images.

TELL ME AWFUL THINGS

I want to know how bad he smells
when you find him.
Did he reek of rotting meat mixed with shit?
Does it haunt you?
Tell me about his decaying body.
How he's bloated and leaking
bloody foam from his mouth.
I want to know what color he is.
Is he turning maroon?
Tell me if his nails and teeth are falling out.
Is he liquefying?
Seeping into the recliner
where he was left.
Suffering.

Tell me awful things.

EXTERMINATOR

R.K. Wolford

Guy next town over
rented the basement to an older woman.
You know the deal–
divorced, down on her luck–
cats, sweatpants, too much Gallo too early.
She paid on time, until she didn't.

After he put the notice in her box,
he smelled the rot.
One skeleton cat ran outside
when he unlocked the door.
Two more were drying on the rug.
He called me and the junkman.

I set the bombs
wherever there was space
in the shoulder-high maze.
I was waiting outside when I heard the crash.
Christ, I thought, there was another cat–

EXTERMINATOR

so I opened the door.

You could see the roaches spinning,
raining from the ceiling in the mist–
then she blundered past me.
She must have hidden
under the piles of trash
when I came in the first time.

On the top step, her foot tore off–
a glistening brown stream ran down the stairs again.
She thrashed for the shadow of the house,
roaches falling from her mouth, her eyes.
They must have burrowed in while she was drunk,
learned to move her from the inside.

I sprayed until my tank was empty,
until she stopped jerking
against the foundation's cinderblocks.
I would have used the can of gas
I keep for yellow jackets,
if they hadn't stopped me.

HABEL

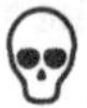

John Smith

This year be that of eighteen forty and three
Of those lost, we beings' unawares
O'er the realm weary, which be most eerie
Made merry by those vows who swear'd
For my bride did I buy a large house
Which dangled high upon a sea cliff
As a castle which befits that of a vassal
Stood this most perfect of wedding-day gifts
So, across the rusty drawbridge we rode
Enthralled over our quaint, little marriage
Know not we, of the dangers that be
Upon leaving our gilded, filigreed carriage
Within this majestic fortification
My bride and I need never to depart
There be ones to scuttle and ones to buttle
About the dreary and weary ramparts
Within these walls arose a splendid spire
That pricked at chastity's gate
Of her care, she begged to share

HADEL

For neither of we could wait
Soon with our passion love quickly came
Exhausted upon the bed we laid
Breathing and sighing, laughing and crying
Being reclined from love's soft serenade

But, in that hoary first night of bliss
Came a dream twixt wild and fraught
A ghost of a man, did come and did stand
To tempt me with what I should naught
His tender lips upon my flesh
Was a hardening and foolish kiss
For women alone, had I only known
Yet, entwined by ropes he did twist
With my lovely bride asleep at my side
Came great trembling, my being understood
Feeling his lust, his longing to thrust
Gave rise to his creepy manhood
His grasping held both fire and ice
Burning and yet cooling was his touch
I did try to scream: "Get out of this dream!"
But could not break his dastardly clutch
This entity knew not of any shame
As I struggled, hoping to awaken
Not to be denied, pass my lips he did glide
Of my body, this ghost hast overtaken

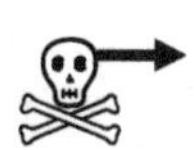

With a forceful groan and besotted moan
Filling my mouth with his ecstasy
Against my muffled pleas of "Just let me be!"
His churning seed was, well, quite tasty
But, this apparition was not yet through
To my horror and to my abject shock
For between my thighs, he mightily pried
And began to assault me buttocks
While my body's instinct being pleasured
This spirit within me was unrelenting
And to my surprise, bubbling did arise
As I lay rapturously unrepenting
Breathing most heavy and hardy
Again, and again, these actions he did repeat
Unable to move, he forcibly continued
Until he felt his needs be complete

Between me and my lovely bride
Rested this bold, ethereal creature
Knowing in my soul that it now had control
As a dominating master and teacher
But as the sun came drifting in
My wife did strive for more satisfaction
Though I be confused, how could I refuse
For she knew not of my phantom's attraction
Thusly, when the specter be not around

HABEL

Fright fills my heart as I knew it would
Such a great distress that she could not redress
Be stirrings none like that old phantasm could
As her discontented time came and went
The more unearthly my body became
Whilst my bride drew cold,
the ghost grew most bold
And I learned of my spooky lover's name
Each night came to be with "Habel" in me
My resistance to him I no longer gave
I came to forget, that I had any regret
As my carnal lust grew albeit depraved
Was this such a wrong and wicked pleasure
Ganymede thought not such of Zeus
For them both found bliss beyond a sweet kiss
As these immortals drunk of each other's juice
Days turned into weeks and weeks into months
And I no longer found me bride so thrilling
Though she wanted to discuss,
she became my disgust
Whilst I craved more lusty specter's drilling
Never said I a word to my bride
Keeping all the torrid horror within me
But late one night, she awoke with a fright
And saw me molested of the entity

Upon the morn, she said, "This shan't be born!"
And tried her best to stab thee with a knife
But my ghost was quicker, the floor even slicker
As he did pull and push to save me life
Swiftly out the window, her angry body flew
Without any wings or means of flight
Did plummet to earth, lacking no dearth
Upon a rocky shore, it did alight
So beneath quiet and still moonbeams
I retrieved the body of my once lovely bride
And carved hieroglyphs into a stone from the cliffs
Hacking her bones so as never, ever to jibe
Condemned to lurch from her immortal perch
Be tormented my late wife each night
To see Habel stroke as well as to poke
Me pleasuring him until dawn's early light
Forevermore comes this tale of lost lore
In the bedchamber, Habel has me chained
Since the love of my life, be not the departed wife
Habel's lust now doth roam unrestrained
Now it can be known and ascribe to the bone
Why Habel's own revenge upon me received
My bride's brother's knife,
took Habel's bloody life
In this castle, his tortured body did bleed
There be only one terror within me now

HABEL

It be not watching of me dearly departed wife
The only fear left, that could cause me bereft
Is if Habel no longer takes hold of my life
When walking this haunted castle by the sea
Some will hear creaks, some will hear moans
Think not they be the torment of me
But that of old Habel pleasuring me bone

JUNG EXPLAINS PIZZA

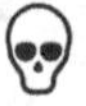

David Shultz

Why pizza is the apex of cuisine—
culinary evolution tapped a primal vein,

you'll eat it cold if you're scavenging
but prefer it arranged warm like a body:

crisp skin of pepperoni and fatty mozzarella
over slick tomato sauce—bloody mess!

The ritual savagery of burnt sacrifice
is ancient history, buried deep-dish deep.

Go on, pull the curving bone of crust,
snap a stretching sinew of cheese.

Now this is communion, digging in a circle
to reconnect with toothy, snarling roots.

Inhaling the fresh fumes of an offering
for our Friday night tribe

BUSY BODY

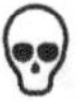

Kurt Newton

Marla was a busy body,
always nosing over neighbor's fences
while pretending to be tending
to her roses
and her daffodils.

Until one hot summer day,
after hours of leering and overhearing,
at the ripe old age of eighty,
Marla fainted dead away,
landing face first in her garden bed.

Sadly, Marla lived alone,
so no one came to her assistance,
and not a single neighbor noticed
she was missing
for quite some time.

Her body lay all but hidden
among the thorny greenery,
still and silent as the elves
that crouched beneath
the ornamental grass.
But on the third day
there was movement,
more a subtle undulation,
a rise and ripple emulating
from the rich carpet underneath.

Marla's hands were the first to exit,
each a slow drag across the soil
like two crabs walking in their sleep.
Her feet then followed,
slippers still attached.

Arms and legs became disjointed,
launching like a small fleet
of pale submarines,
nosing through the begonias
into a sea of lavender.

Marla's head tipped and rolled,
and came to rest alongside
the Grandma's Garden stone,

while parts and pieces disseminated
to every corner of the fenced in yard.

Soon, Marla was more busy than ever,
creeping up toward the sun,
reaching through the fence cracks
into the neighboring yards
her eyesight never better.

Look, there was Rose, her petals spread.
Oh, no, the gardener held
a pair of scissors, grabbed her stem
with leather gloves,
and cut off her head.

Next up was Violet, always shrinking,
shrinking from the trimming,
the stripping, the cutting,
the clipping, trapped inside
the garden fence.

Marla knew what she had to do,
once she reached them,
she would teach them how to tangle,
to strangle, to choke,
and how to take back control.

UGLY SISTER

Joanna Koch

When I plunge the knife
your throat gushes regret.
Oh unwed prince offering a slipper,
your invitation never fits.
A woman of greater grace
might bow or waltz away.
Not me—I wear the damn thing.

Heel, toe, sole chopped.
Soul stuffed into the shape
of the expectation of kings
beginning another stolen proposal.
I'll have you, by Medusa's will.

This time, you will not ignore me.
You will not choose the blonde.
You will not wear a woman
like an accessory. You can comply
or die. Be my muse or you lose.

UGLY SISTER

I'll choose which choice parts.

For too long, princes played me.
A plush toy with detachable bits:
John took the clitoris, David ate the brain,
Chris swallowed the stuffing.
Pink plush labia, green plush bile,
fat feet forced into stilettos,
sling backs, thigh-highs, and pumps.
My soft body un-seamed, spilling out tufts.

The bloodletting behind the glass
slipper is civic. China doll blondes
showcase blue veins below porcelain skin—
rivers of submission dam under ice.
Crass as a Chinese Elm, my veins run hot.
Ropey red, straining against dark skin,
hirsute, marred, too opaque to confuse
the character with the costume—
I bleed, bleed, and burst.

When I plunge my knife,
your mouth gushes regret.
White-hot porcelain lies pour
from the holes in your neck.
Molten glass drool puddles,

molds to the shape of my cloven-plush feet—
you melt into a seamless liquid fit.
You harden—cool, you slip on and off with ease.
Ruined, you cling too tight.
Must I now chew off my own legs
to escape your caring snare?

BONFIRE

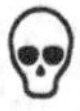

Christopher Woods

She was burning in the field, in the high grass already flaring. She had transgressed, served his Hungry Man dinner lukewarm again. He was already at a breaking point, job all fizzled out, kids crying for Happy Meals. It was too much. So he had driven her from the house of ordinary horrors to the free, wide expanse beneath the stars where he trussed her, like his Pappy had taught him. She couldn't move, couldn't speak with her panties—relics of a final love of a kind, in her mouth. Only her eyes remained, and he was tired of them too. So, he set her aflame as planned, and as he walked away, he looked back over his shoulder at his work: the smoke beginning to rise into the dark sky near the strip center on the highway, felt nothing but the joy of vengeance for every last sin she had committed.

ALONE IN THE LAND OF ROBOTS

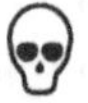

Shaun Avery

I didn't care when the robots
Killed the rest of mankind
I was the last human
But I didn't really mind
No, I just sat there
Living online from my room
Watching through the window
As this land became a tomb

Then they started cleaning up
And I wondered, *why me?*
I couldn't work out why
The robots had let me go free
So I staggered from my house
For the first time in years
I walked out into the sunlight
And finally faced all my fears

AL°NE IN THE LAND °F R°B°TS

This area's head robot came up
Armed with guns and metal whip
I said, "hey, dude, what's happening?
What's going on with this?"
It muttered something mechanical
I didn't understand
But then another one came behind me
And took hold of my hand

I turned around to face it
Saw a skin-based machine
Something almost human
If you get what I mean
A female, yes, she told me:
"You must be confused
Come and sit down with me
And I'll show you the news"

Yes, they had their own news now
They'd taken over the TV
They were broadcasting all around the world
Those clever damn machines
But they were talking all about me
And she could see that I was stunned
So she started to explain
Just what the robots had done

“You never left your room” she said
“You were always in a screen
At a computer or on your tablet
Never with another human being
That makes you more us than them
Do you finally see?
Now I want you to stand up
And come on home with me”

I did like she told me
And she carried me to bed
She’d picked out a home for us
That was what she said
And there we lay together
Her fingers cold at first then warm
But as I slid so deep inside her
Something new and great was born

That was how it started
How we slowly fell in love
She’d been built to pleasure humans
And I couldn’t get enough
But we talked for ages, too
And the story that she told
Was of a whole new world
One the robots would now mould

And I guess that was where I went wrong
I grew a little bit too bold
I wanted to see that world with her
Before I got too old
"Where would you like to go?"
She asked me one night in our bed
"Somewhere strange and weird, darling"
That was what I said

She said "okay" and we flew
Inside a giant carrier droid
We went to some place mystical
A place long since destroyed
But not just by the robots
Though they had done their bit
No, a land mostly ruined
From something else: magic

But we didn't believe in that
And that was our mistake
I was crouched down by an old man
When he quickly came awake
And grabbed my hand
And muttered something in a foreign tongue
Laughed and then collapsed and died
Spitting blood up from his lungs

My love ran to me
And placed her hand on mine
Wondered, "are you okay?"
And I told her I was fine
But inside I felt a fever
A tingling in my blood
And when she said, "let's go home now"
I agreed we should

I wondered what was wrong
The fever building as we flew home
Something was in my body
Something deadly yet unknown
And as we walked into our house
My love paused and then collapsed
And somewhere all around me
I heard the dead man as he laughed
"You traitor," he seemed to say

"You choose them over us
Now here comes your punishment
Watch your new brethren start to rust"
But first I sat down with my love
Saw the energy in her die
Then I screamed up to the heavens
And in despair ran outside

ALONE IN THE LAND OF ROBOTS

I was thinking of all the flying robots
We'd crossed across the sky
Our carrier was friendly
Always stopped to tell them "hi"
And my love, she had touched him
And he in turn touched them
That was when I knew my newfound race
Was now truly condemned

So I sat and watched the news
Saw that it was indeed worldwide
A constant running commentary
As the robot race, they died
But could this truly come from me?
I was filled with doubt
Until the man's ghost appeared
And he spelt it all out

"I worked on the curse before they came"
That was what he said
"I didn't have much time
The rest of the village was dead
I needed to touch a robot
To transfer from skin to steel
But they shot me from afar
So the curse remained in me

"Until you arrived," he added
Saying it with a grin
"I put the curse in your flesh
The spell inside your skin
And then with just one touch
I saw you pass it to your mate
From her onto the next and next
And that sealed the robots' fate"

"But how come you didn't die?"
That was what I had to know
"I mean, how long has it been?
"The robots rose so long ago"
"Too much rage in me to die"
He said full of hate
"My powers told me you would come
I just had to wait"

Then he vanished, and I wept
Curled up on the floor
In the dead arms of my love
I wished for just one chance more
But from her hybrid remains
Came no reply, not a groan
I was alone in the land of robots
But now I'm just alone

ABOMINATION

Jordan Paris

The wedding we see, and the wedding that they do, are two different things.
I mean,
we can all agree that
a variety of bricks and ivy have collided perfectly
to make the church
that my husband and I
are today forever intertwined by—
the father,
son,
and holy ghost.
However,
it seems to only be us that notices how gallons of coagulated blood creep between the ivy and
ancient basis of existence, supporting each little thing that has formed this home. This place.
Us.
Our surroundings are seemingly stuck together by sacrifice and the sinew of raw flesh,

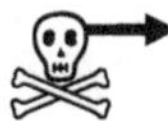

untouched and smelly and disgusting,
shaking to the beat of
broken bones and beaten bodies
we are left downtrodden, bloodied, looking amongst
the battle of society that fights now to understand
the wedding.
They see two men—just two men.
An accepting world, because we are getting married.
That's what they see—that's all that matters.
But I look at him, and I see
for a flickering moment
what the waiting has taken from us.
A body who has silently, and not so silently,
been beaten,
paraded around and prized for his body by sad,
sad people.
I watch the crimson trickle from his lips, draining out on-
to his suit—cleanly onto my white
one as we hold each other close—so close.
The blood drying, gluing our bodies together in a way
that the priest may never know,
because he doesn't see
no one does.
His beautiful, beautiful rainbow suit in this horrible world
is battered and beaten and bloodied
and breaking,

with little shards of his broken heart decorating his
sleeves as if to wear his brokenness on his
shoulders, as if he is proud.
Because the ones who did it to us, they are proud.
but we must be prouder.
The words bubble through his bloody lips, "I do."
and in the moment before his lips touch mine I see my
own reflection in those beautiful, sane eyes
and look into my own insane ones.
The most ugly,
most horrific,
most obliterating wrong thing,
is knowing that his parents,
the ones front and center of the crowd,
are silently throwing us daggers. I try to catch for so long
but
when he kisses me,
I let my guard down—
he deserves that—
we deserve that.
the last and final blow catches me in the heart, as soon as
my lips touch his.
It is done.
I fall to his feet, with the sound of blood dropping to the
cement around me. And I swear,
I swear...I can hear cheers.

ONE GLASS EYE

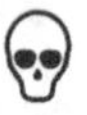

North Adam

Grunt, crunch, grunt, out in the pen.
His ceiling fan whirrs, ruffles his sister's curls,
She sleeps on, safe and warm in her favorite blue dress.

Grunt, crunch, grunt, out in the pen.
The scum gurgles, noisy and rude and alive.
Too alive for Abel's taste.

Shut up, he barks at the window.
His too-slow hand slaps one glass eye.
Across the workbench (*merrily—merrily—merrily*),
It rolls fast.
Faster than his too-slow hand, faster than a thought.
Fast little runner like Abel's sister was.

ONE GLASS EYE

It's lodged stubborn and deep in the cracks.
Can’t (*won’t*) be pried out.
Grunt, crunch, grunt, inside and outside.
It glints, winks at him from beneath the floorboards.
Stubborn, just like her.

No more gurgles. His sister sleeps on.
Abel smiles.
“Sleep well.” The ceiling fan croaks, whirrs.
Abel picks up the remaining glass eye,
Chocolate-sable-dirt brown like hers.

One glass eye watches him work.

THE HOUSE ON THE HILL

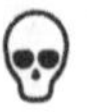

Michael Meroney

There was a house,
a house on the hill.
The memories it gave me,
they do plague me still.

Images and hauntings—
I just can't forget.
Each night that I lie down
I wake up in a sweat.

So many lives
and as many deaths.
All loving families,
crushed bodies and breaths.

Neighbors and friends
that perished in gore.
Seen through the windows,
heard through the door.

THE H°USE °N THE HILL

They all made the papers
and tales they were spun.
Though once there were many
now there are none.

The first was a family
from Boston, I think.
The dad had an accent
and he sure loved to drink.

He battered his wife
and his children, they wept
One arctic night
this family, they slept

The man, maybe from Boston,
he stood over each bed.
With laughter erupting,
took an axe to each head.

He sat on the lawn,
with a smile on his face.
Stark naked and raving,
said they polluted his space.

One thing would stay with me
that I found rather odd,
when quoted of his crime
the man cried he was God.

Now things were made right
since his family was dead.
"The work of the devil
was rapid," he said.

A drunken made terror
the authorities did claim.
Several weeks later
things went back to the same.

But the town they did whisper,
this house it was cursed.
A legend was born
that took a turn for the worst.

It all made me wonder,
but life did go on.
The next family moved in
and the evil did spawn.

THE HOUSE ON THE HILL

I knew the youngest
had seen her at school.
She had no friends—
people thought her a ghoul.

She lived in “that place”
where the people had died
and the naked man sat,
his axe by his side.

This new family came,
a great deal they were offered.
All that I knew
was their last name was Crawford.

I wouldn’t listen
to the others at school—
I said hi to the girl
that to some was a ghoul.

My kindness was spurned—
the girl she seemed weird.
She would mutilate her family;
on the wall, blood was smeared.

Their intestines she ate—
cooked in an oven.
The town branded her a witch,
but where was her coven?

They locked her away—
she was crazy, they knew it.
The last words she would speak
"God made me do it."

The neighbors, they hushed,
but they never forgot.
And the house would be left,
abandoned to rot.

It sat there for years—
too many to tell.
Dead to the world,
coming with it the smell.

Then many years later
an eccentric old man
purchased the property
as part of his plan.

THE HOUSE ON THE HILL

To have him a dream house
this he had said,
but that which would follow
was a nightmare instead.

For a while things were quiet—
not a mention was made.
Still people did wonder
what went on in the shade.

An answer was given
one Christmas Day morning—
a holiday of horror
that came without warning.

Screams there were heard
of most blood curdling variety
over at the house
of such vast notoriety.

Upon clustered arrival
only silence was heard.
The door was wide open,
the next moments were blurred.

Rumors were spoken
from a gathering mass.
Findings that which caused them
to vomit in the grass.

The house was filled
with a stench that was horrid.
Though winter raged on
inside temperatures were torrid.

Body parts were found
in each of the rooms,
severed and decayed,
all to choke on the fumes.

There was blood on the walls,
ceilings and floors—
the windows all blackened—
there were crosses on the doors.

"A house made of God"
the man confessed—
then lead away
no one to clean up the mess.

THE HOUSE ON THE HILL

The bodies were women—
thieving and harlot,
purveyors of filth—
now mangled in scarlet.

Purity and virtue
were his ultimate goals.
He cut out their hearts
to free all of their souls.

When the papers reported,
the house became still,
abandoned forever,
left to rot on that hill.

After all there was no one
who could wish to reside
in a hall reeked with presence
of those who had died.

Still I admit,
curious must I be—
if inside I would sneak.
What at night would I see?

There, something was with me,
amidst all the rubble.
And like a bat out of Hell
I flew from the trouble.

Literally of hell.
This I surmised:
a few trips to the library
colored me surprised.

The house had been built
on once hallowed ground.
A place that of worship
then burnt to the mound.

On the earth soaked with pestilence
four walls were erected
and to the evil it begat—
the town was affected.

Though never again
would it be home unto person.
All around would be damned
as conditions did worsen.

THE HOUSE ON THE HILL

There was talk of a presence
on the streets did prowl.
The air smelled of death
and the wind it did howl.

In the night as I slumbered,
amongst prisoned eyes
a commotion arose
with flames in the skies.

What mysteries behind us
now never to know.
The house burnt to the ground
now a vacant plateau.

All the years later,
still I am haunted.
My existence left tainted,
my sleep it now taunted.

As my mind it lay dormant
and the air be it still
the whispers become screams—
no house, only hill.

SILENT ENEMIES

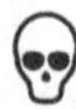

Brian James Lewis

There are days when
all I want to do is
kill myself

Wash away the pain
forever and just
be totally free

Of what I've become
fat and addicted to drugs
meant to manage my

Pain but they only
dull it a little and
turn my brain to sludge

Then drive me crazy
because my face itches
like it is full of a

SILENT ENEMIES

Million tiny bugs
that are trying to eat
the inside of my nose

I wipe and wash
scratch and poke
but it's no use

Damn it!
I just want a razor
sharp knife so I can

Peel away the
skin of my face in
thin bloody sheets

Just to get rid
of the maddening itch
the crawling prickle

That keeps me awake
at two in the morning
ruining any chance

Of sleep—my dreams
invaded by the horrible
sensations that rule me

Pain pulses and
flares, forcing me
out of my own bed

To face the itching
that make one's
fingers enemies that

Attack in the night—
like silent killers—
from another realm.

AUTOPSY

Detroit Kallunki

My thoughts are soft as snow
small and cold and rabbit-white
virtually soundless
in the emptiness of the night
but your words are like a thunderstorm
crashing and booming and dark and magnetic
with large jolts of electricity
and you can't hear me
when I beg you to stop
or maybe
you just pretend not to hear the snow
because you think the rain is more important

and the blistering heat of your touch
and your heavy and hard grip
is too rough and cuts into me too deeply
and I bleed fire and you lap it up and want more
so you do it again
over

and
over
you are a desert on my cold skin
and i don't like it
so
I
try
to
squirm
away

dismantle me
take me apart
the way I know you want to
hold me down and
gut me like a fish
slice me cleanly from my throat to my toes
expose my insides to the world
let everyone see
the things held within
ignore me when I beg you to:
stop
please
don't
no

AUT°PSY

grab fistfuls of my squirming intestines
Pull them out and set them down
so they can slither about and listen to you charm them
like snakes
pick at my bones
play them like a xylophone
drum on them with your fingers
rearrange everything
until it sits where you want it to

wear my heart on your sleeve
spurting and dripping and oozing
oxygenated
scarlet
blood
all over your white shirt
pull my teeth out of my mouth
they would make beautiful ornaments
peel my fingertips and cuticles back
until my nails fall off
tickle my brain through the cracks in my skull
the ones you made
because the pressure was too strong in my head
use my eyes as pincushions
scoop them out of my head with a spoon
and stab them all over

with teeny tiny needles
you've already damaged me beyond repair
so why not tear me apart at the seams
and make me the puppet you've always wished for me
to be

THIS PAGE IS INTENTIONALLY LEFT BLANK

HIDDEN

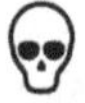

Shannon Elizabeth

Ink and Acrylic on Paper

2019

HIDDEN

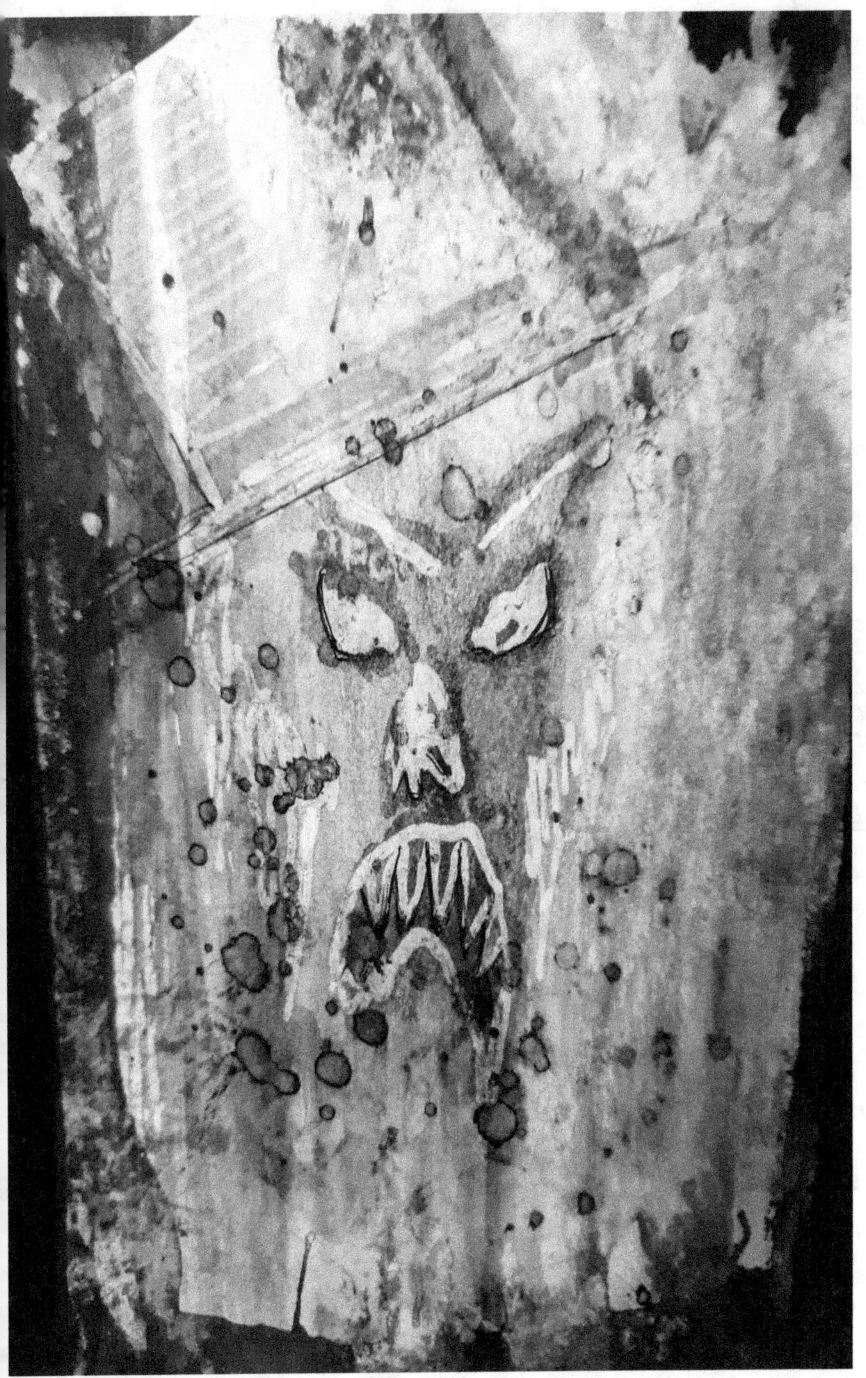

THE ARTIST

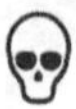

John Andrews

As I write this story,
cutting into your flesh,
I taste your blood,
gushing, fresh.

Upon the floor,
a pool of red.
Behind a locked door,
soon to be dead.

Close your eyes, my love,
I make you a piece of art.
As I cut myself—
my blood with yours to start.

I am the artist,
don't you see?
I have the floor—
turn the lights upon your body with glee.

THE ARTIST

A puzzling piece,
red lined sliced.
Wined and dined—
our precious blood entwined

THE LITTLEST MURDER

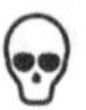

Christina Digan

Blood and brains in the foyer,
A lifeless corpse by the stairs.
Its intestines pulled from the gaping wound
and wrapped around the bannister

The carpet is filled with blood
sticky and coagulated.
A murderer came to pay a visit
and a family of 7 have perished.

The father tried to be brave,
He came at her with an ax.
The plan was quickly reversed
and his brains now reside on the mantle.

A hacksaw was used, Grandma and Grandpa lay dead,
their heads split down the middle.
Grandma's head is now floating
in the oatmeal she was stirring.

THE LITTLEST MURDER

Grandpa lay in the sun room
his body bloated and stiff;
eyes wide, an expression of shock
down the middle, his skull split.

The twins lay upstairs
In their beds where they slept:
one tied to the bedposts,
the other curled in a ball.

Their torsos were sliced open,
a hack job for sure!
Their intestines were pulled
and wrapped together for eternity.

The house was a grind scene
who could do such a thing?
But wait! There's one missing:
the little girl of age ten.

An amber alert is issued,
a kidnapping for sure.
They must find the killer,
they must save the child.

She is apprehended on I-24—
by the side of the road,
her gingham dress covered in blood,
her hands dirty from fight.

Fingernails are analyzed,
the results are soon in:
the skin under her nails
matches her Dad's DNA.

How is that possible they wonder,
What role did she play?
The little girl just smiles,
and watches them try to comprehend.

They ask for her statement,
she gives tale of horror and gore.
They can't believe what they are hearing,
she was the murderer all along.

She explains the night of the crime,
one detail at a time.
Her blue eyes cold and unfeeling.
her voice low and even.

THE LITTLEST MURDER

"I wanted ice cream," she said.
They all had to die—
sick of her brothers—
Daddy too stupid.

Grandpa too old and cranky,
she made sure they felled,
bound to be the corpse—
for ice cream, putrid.

BIBLIOGRAPHY

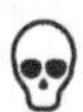

Licensed Usage

IMAGES

Cortes, Fernando. "Depression, Man with His Eyes Fixed on Holders—Image." *Shutterstock*, ID: 212180260, https://www.shutterstock.com/image-photo/depression-man-his-eyes-fixed-on-212180260?src=library. Accessed 19 July, 2019.

GRAPHICS

NAS. "Alien, Head, Pirate, Skull, Walker, Zombie Icon." *Iconfinder*, https://www.iconfinder.com/icons/548329alien_head_pirate_skull_walker_zombie_icon. Accessed 1 July, 2019

FONTS

Curtis, Nick and Nelsson, Roger. "Copasetic NF Pro." *My Fonts*, https://www.myfonts.com/fonts/cheapprofonts/copasetic-nf-pro. CheapProFonts: 6 May, 2009. Accessed 1 July, 2019.

Free Commercial Usage

Rakowski, David. "Upper East Side." *Font Squirrel*, 7 Oct. 2009, https://www.fontsquirrel.com/fonts/uppereastside. Accessed 1 July, 2019.

ABOUT THE EDITORS

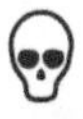

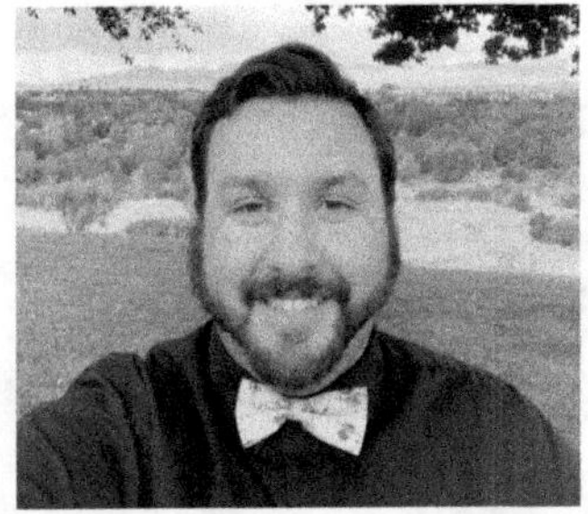

Daniel Cureton is a writer, editor, publisher, and avant-garde poet. He holds an MA in English from Weber State University. He currently lives in Salt Lake City, UT with his cat Oliver, a cross eyed Siamese.

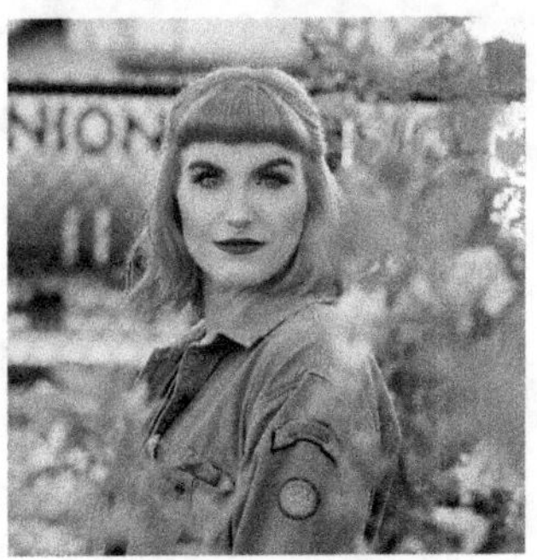

Kylie Williamson has been a guest editor for *Strange Stories* and participated in putting together *Metaphor* at Weber State University, where she currently teaches while pursuing her MA in English.

NOTES

www.ingramcontent.com/pod-product-compliance
Lightning Source LLC
Chambersburg PA
CBHW060548310726
48982CB00008B/1054/J

* 9 7 8 1 7 3 4 0 0 6 7 2 8 *